KINNICK CAMPBELL

Three Years of Learning to Be Enough

One Day, One Recipe

Second edition

ISBN (paperback): 979-8-9995510-2-3
ISBN (hardcover): 979-8-9995510-4-7

Editing by Todd Campbell, Ph.D.
Advisor: Rosie Cote-Landry
Cover art by Randi-Lyn Whitneck

This book was professionally typeset on Reedsy.
Find out more at reedsy.com

For the kid I used to be –
who stayed quiet to keep the peace,
who baked to feel safe,
and who thought love had to be earned through perfection.

For anyone who's ever felt like too much or not enough –
you are worthy, you are soft and strong, and you are not alone.

Contents

Read This First

Hey. Before you dive in, I'd like to offer you a moment of softness.

This book is personal. It holds stories about growing up, coming out, breaking down, starting over, and all the complicated, tender feelings in between. Along the way, it touches on mental health, burnout, disordered eating, identity, and what it means to feel like you're not enough.

I've done my best to write with honesty, care, and gentleness – not to overwhelm you, but to connect with the part of you that just needs to feel seen. Still, I know that some moments may feel heavy. If they do, it's okay to pause. Skip a chapter. Take a breath. Come back later – or not at all. There's no right way to read this book. Take it at your own pace. Take what you need. Leave the rest.

This isn't a survival guide. It's not a how-to. It's a collection of real moments, layered with flour and fear and healing and hope. I wrote it for the version of me who needed it – and maybe for you, too. If your life feels like it's not rising the way you hoped, I promise: that doesn't mean you've failed. It just means you're still becoming.

And becoming takes time. You are not broken. You are not behind. You are NOT alone.

Introduction

Why I Wrote This

This isn't a perfect cookbook – and it's definitely not a perfect life.

It's a little messy, a little sweet, and – more than anything – I hope it feels like a place to breathe. I wrote this for the ones who feel like they're falling apart. For the people who are exhausted from trying to hold it all together. For anyone who feels unseen, stuck, or like they've lost their way. If that's you, you're not alone.

Life has a way of pulling us in every direction. Some days rise beautifully. Others sink in the middle. And sometimes, no matter how carefully you follow the steps, things still fall apart. But that doesn't mean you're broken. It just means you're human. And you can still become who you're meant to be.

I think about the first fundraiser I ever hosted. I stayed up late the night before, carefully piping cream puffs – nervous, hopeful, doing everything the recipe told me to. But when I opened the oven door, they had collapsed entirely. I was crushed. I thought I failed. But people still ordered. They still donated. They still cared. That night taught me something I've held onto ever since: even when things don't rise the way you hoped, you still can.

This book is a collection of stories and recipes, each one paired together for a reason. The recipes aren't just here for fun (though I hope you bake them). They reflect what I was going through, symbolically and emotionally.

You'll find a chapter about perfectionism and burnout, paired with an overbaked chocolate chip cookie: something that looks fine on the outside but is dry and brittle underneath. There's a story about feeling like I wasn't enough, followed by a cracked cake that still tastes good. And another chapter explores what it meant to slow down and rebuild, mirrored by a simple, slow-rise bread recipe that taught me to trust the process.

These aren't polished stories, just honest ones. You'll read about coming out, struggling with school, trying to be everything for everyone, rediscovering joy through friendship, chasing big dreams, and burning out hard. And with each moment, something from the kitchen that helped me make sense of it all.

You can read this book from start to finish or jump to whatever chapter feels right. Whether you're here for the recipes, the stories, or just a little reassurance that someone else gets it, I hope you find warmth in these pages.

To protect the people in these stories, I've changed all names and identifying details. But the emotions, the memories, and the lessons – they're all mine.

So why now? Because I'm ready. Because I believe stories are meant to be shared. Because someone out there might need to hear this the way I once did. I want you to know – it's okay. It's OK to fall apart. It's OK to be tired. It's OK to take life one day at a time. It's OK not to have all the answers.

I'm still figuring it out, too. These days, I'm just taking things slowly – working towards my goals, baking when I need to breathe, and learning to appreciate the imperfect in both life and dough. And maybe, that's enough.

So, if your cream puffs fall flat, or your life feels like it's not rising quite right, start here. Let this be a soft place to land.

Take what you need. A sugar-dusted recipe. A little hope. And if all else fails – bake something warm. It helps more than you'd think.

Chapter 1: Sweet on the Inside

It was December 2022, the start of winter break, and our house smelled like cinnamon, sugar cookies, and whatever scent was in the tart warmer that week. My siblings were laughing downstairs with my parents, the fireplace was crackling, and Wii Golf was loud enough to echo through the walls. The tree glowed with colored lights and years of collected ornaments. It was cozy. It was cheerful. It should have felt perfect.

But I was upstairs, curled up in my room with the slanted ceiling, the one that didn't smell like anything. I wasn't baking, even though I loved to bake. I wasn't watching movies, even though I loved those too. I was texting Miles – a boy I'd met at school. He was sweet, funny, out. He made my chest tighten every time he texted back. Even while he was on vacation in the South, we talked every day. I was scared to ruin it. I was afraid to say too much, but I also wanted to say everything.

I had known for a while – I was gay. But no one else knew. Not my family. Not even Miles. And in that moment, while the house buzzed with warmth downstairs, I felt alone in a room that felt more like a closet than a bedroom. Not just physically, but emotionally. I wanted to be downstairs. I wanted to be present. But I also wanted to be texting Miles under the covers, letting myself feel the one thing I was always trying to suppress: softness.

That was what I was craving most – to feel soft and not be punished for it.

I watched my brother joke about his girlfriend. I watched my parents smile at the thought of their kids growing up and pairing off. And I kept thinking, 'I want that too.' I want what they have – but with someone like Miles. I imagined introducing him to my family, decorating a tree together, and laughing over burnt cookies. I imagined being out and being honest. But mostly, I imagined being safe.

Every time I thought about telling them, I stopped myself. I didn't want to ruin anything – the holiday, the mood, their image of me. So instead, I put on my usual sweater, pushed up my nerd glasses, and sat in silence. Even my Christmas ornament that year felt wrong – just another object that didn't reflect who I actually was. I remember baking puppy chow one night, chocolate and powdered sugar clinging to my fingers, and realizing how peaceful that moment felt. Baking was the one space where I didn't have to hide, where I could express something without saying anything.

But outside the kitchen, I was shrinking. I filtered my laugh. Adjusted my voice and changed how I walked. In middle school, I told people I liked girls because I thought I had to. Now, I just avoided the question altogether. Even when people asked, "Are you gay?" – I always deflected. I was afraid they already knew. Afraid they'd stop looking at me the same way. Afraid of being a disappointment.

Because that was the word that haunted me most: disappointment. I wasn't afraid of being hated. I was worried that if I said the truth, I'd lose something I couldn't get back.

And then one night, I couldn't hold it anymore.

The house was dark. Everyone was asleep. I was shaking as I walked into my parents' room. I stepped through the cracked door, trembling, and said the words that had lived in me for far too long.

"I'm gay. I'm sorry. But this is who I am. And nothing can change that."

I was already crying. I barely remember what they said – only that my mom tried to relate. She said she thought girls were cute, but she didn't like them like that. She tried to compare our experiences. I wanted to scream, 'You don't understand.' You never have. But I didn't say that. I just kept crying. They told me they loved me, but also told me I could "do what I want" once I turned eighteen, which meant: not now. Not here. Not while I'm under their roof.

I walked out of the room, crushed. Not because they yelled. But because their love felt like it had limits. But a few days later, in a car ride to get haircuts, my brothers looked at me and said they already knew. They told me they were sorry Mom was like this and shared how they loved me anyway. They helped me understand how my Mom and Dad were raised in Christian homes at a different time and would need more time to process what I'd shared, but assured me of their love. My brothers asked for no edits. No conditions. Just love. That moment, quiet and simple, was the first time I felt like maybe I wasn't alone.

And I told Miles.

I told him I liked him, more than just a friend. I sent the message, heart pounding, ready to regret it. But he surprised me in the best way. He was kind. Gentle. Blushy. After that, I started using emojis I'd usually delete. I called him a cutie. I flirted the way I always wanted to. I didn't hide behind jokes. I didn't overthink every word.

It was terrifying. But it also felt like breathing. For the first time in forever, I didn't feel like I had to rehearse being myself. I still wasn't safe everywhere. But I was no longer invisible – and that changed everything.

I wore my crystal bracelets – the ones my mom once said were "for girls." I didn't take them off. I stopped shrinking myself in conversations. I let my voice soften. I let my laugh stay.

I whispered to myself: It's okay. You don't have to apologize for softness anymore.

And slowly, the way I saw myself began to shift. I realized I was layered – soft, afraid, bold, becoming, just like the things I loved to bake. I used to think I had to strip those layers away to be accepted. But now, I was starting to believe I could keep them.

Recipe: Pumpkin Spice Linzer Cookies

Why This Recipe

These cookies feel like that winter break – layered, soft, and just delicate enough to fall apart if you press too hard. Linzer cookies are built on contrast: tender edges, warm spice, and a hidden sweetness in the middle. They're not flashy. They're not perfect. But if you take your time, you end up with something whole.

That's what I was craving then – softness that didn't need to be hidden, sweetness that didn't have to be earned. I wasn't ready to say much out loud, but I could still make something that held what I was feeling. This recipe reminds me of that: of learning that it's okay to be a little messy, a little cracked, and still completely worth holding together.

Ingredients

Cookies:

- 1 cup unsalted butter, softened (226 g)
- 1 ¼ cups powdered sugar (150 g)
- 2 egg yolks
- 1 tsp vanilla extract
- 2 ½ cups all-purpose flour (300 g)
- 1 cup almond meal (100 g)
- ½ tsp allspice
- ½ tsp cinnamon
- ½ tsp nutmeg
- ½ tsp fine salt

Pumpkin Jam:

- 1 (29 oz.) can pumpkin pureé
- 1 ½ cups orange juice (355 mL)

- 1 packet fruit pectin
- 1 tsp ground ginger
- ½ tsp nutmeg
- ½ tsp cloves
- 1 ½ tsp cinnamon
- 4 ½ cups granulated sugar (900 g)
- 2 tbsp lemon juice (30 mL)
- 4 tbsp cornstarch (32 g)
- 4 tbsp cold water (60 mL)

Royal Icing:

- 4 cups powdered sugar (480 g)
- 4 tbsp meringue powder (32 g)
- 1/2 cup plus 2 tbsp (150 mL) room temperature water
- Gel food coloring

Directions

For the Cookies:

1. Cream the butter and powdered sugar until the mixture is light and fluffy.
2. Add egg yolk and vanilla; beat until incorporated.
3. In a separate bowl, whisk together flour, almond meal, allspice, cinnamon, nutmeg, and salt.
4. Gradually add the dry mixture to the egg mixture, one tablespoon at a time.
5. Gently knead the dough until it forms a soft ball.
6. Divide the dough into two parts. Roll each one between baking paper to a thickness of 2–3 mm.

7. Refrigerate both sheets for 1 to 2 hours.
8. Cut out half of the cookies as complete rounds and the other half with center cut-outs (for the Linzer sandwich tops). Chill cut cookies for at least 1 hour.
9. Preheat the oven to 355°F (180 °C).
10. Line baking trays with parchment paper. Place cookies on the trays, spacing them about 1 inch apart.
11. Bake for 8-12 minutes, or until the edges are lightly golden.
12. Let the cookies cool completely on the trays before assembling and decorating.

For the Pumpkin Jam:

1. In a large pot, combine the pumpkin pureé, orange juice, pectin, ginger, nutmeg, cloves, and cinnamon. Warm over medium heat, stirring often, until the mixture is hot and the pectin is dissolved.
2. Stir in the sugar and lemon juice until fully incorporated.
3. Raise the heat to medium-high and bring the mixture to a rolling boil, stirring constantly. Boil for 1 minute to activate the pectin.
4. In a small bowl, whisk together the cornstarch and cold water until completely smooth.
5. Reduce the heat so the jam is gently simmering. Slowly pour in the cornstarch slurry while stirring constantly.
6. Cook for 3-4 minutes stirring constantly, until the jam becomes thick and glossy.
7. Remove from heat and let cool on the counter for about 30 minutes.
8. Spoon into a bowl and refrigerate for at least 1 hour, or until fully set.

Note: This jam thickens as it chills.

Extra: Store any leftover pumpkin jam in a sealed mason jar in the refrigerator for up to 1 week.

For the Royal Icing:

1. Beat all ingredients for 2 minutes with a mixer.
2. Add more water (1 tbsp at a time) for thinner icing. Mix longer for thicker icing.

Note: The royal icing will typically set fully in 4-6 hours at room temperature. For best results, let the decorated cookies sit overnight.

To Assemble:

1. Spread a spoonful of pumpkin jam on the flat side of each full cookie round.
2. Gently press a cut-out cookie on top to create a sandwich, allowing the jam to show through the center.
3. Decorate the tops with royal icing, piping, flooding, or simply drizzling as desired.
4. Let the cookies rest at room temperature until the icing is fully set.

Personal Note

I made these on October 23, 2024, for the Spooky Cut-Out Cookies Bake-Off hosted by the Connecticut Restaurant Association. They weren't perfect – some cracked, some spread too much – but I still loved them.

Chapter 2: Burnt at the Edges

It was early 2024, still winter, though the air outside had started to soften, like it was thinking about spring. Inside, the house was the same as always: drafty around the edges, never great at holding heat, but still cozy in the ways that mattered. My mom's 1800s-style home had its own kind of warmth – dim lighting, old wood floors.

That night, the four of us – me, my parents, and my older brother – were in the living room. The TV was on, playing some show I didn't recognize, but no one was really watching. Everyone seemed relaxed. The energy felt easy, familiar.

I was still in my school clothes – jeans and a crewneck – curled into the corner of the couch. But inside, something felt different. Lighter. I'd just finished Bakeshop 1 the semester before and was midway through Bakeshop 2. Somewhere between powdered sugar, overmixed dough, and the hum of the ovens, I had realized something: I wanted to be a pastry chef.

Not just for fun. Not as a side thing. I wanted this to be my life.

It felt a little foolish to admit out loud. I'd always imagined more "practical" futures – maybe the medical field, or early childhood education. As my dad worked at the University of Connecticut (UConn), I had the option to attend tuition-free. However, they didn't offer a culinary arts program. If I followed this dream, it would mean going somewhere else and not taking advantage of the free tuition. Choosing a path no one in my family – none of my four siblings, no one we knew – had ever taken.

And yet, I wasn't afraid. Not really. This was the first time something felt clear, like it fit. Like it was mine. I didn't rehearse what I was going to say.

I just said it, leaning slightly forward, like getting the words out would help them land the right way.

"I think I have an idea of something I might want to do for a job."

They looked over – curious, attentive. I mean, I'm their son. Of course, they wanted to know. There was a pause. Not an uncomfortable one, just long enough to let the words sink in. I felt calm. Hopeful. I wasn't asking for permission – I just wanted them to see it, too.

That night, the dream felt simple and bright. Like something good was beginning. But excitement doesn't always stay excitement – not when it meets expectations head-on. And pretty soon, that bright dream started to feel like something I had to carry just right, or risk dropping everything.

When I told my parents I wanted to be a pastry chef, their response was practical, immediate, and heavy: I should just go to UConn. There were so many majors there, they said – so many paths to explore. Why throw away free tuition for something that seemed so specific? So impractical? I fought back- not angrily, just honestly. What if this is really what I want to do?

They reminded me that they were limited in what they could do financially with college, and that if I chose a school other than UConn, it would mean taking on student loans. They asked where this dream came from. It felt like they needed a justification I couldn't fully explain yet – something beyond just "it makes me happy."

Eventually, they came around. They let me bake almost whenever I wanted. They said they'd support me, even if they disagreed with my choice. "We're your parents," they said. "Of course, we'll support you."

But their support came with terms. They told me I'd need to get excellent grades – a strong SAT score. Apply for as many scholarships as I could. They didn't ask me to work – they actually said I shouldn't. But I took on a job anyway. Because I thought that's what I needed to do.

I told myself that if I wanted this dream badly enough, I had to prove it. That people wouldn't take me seriously unless I worked for it – literally. I didn't want to feel like I was asking for too much. I wanted to earn it, even if no one was asking me to.

So in March, just after my birthday, I applied at TJ Maxx, a retail store, and got hired. The job was minimum wage and stressful. Most nights, I worked from 4 or 5 until 9:45, came home drained, and still had homework to finish. I drank a Celsius energy drink before almost every shift – just to stay upright.

School was just as intense. I was already in honors classes last year, and this year I added three college-level ones. Homework piled up fast. On top of that, I was still leading the Connecticut Association of Student Councils (CASC) – first as the Eastern District Coordinator, and now as President. I was writing speeches, running meetings, and planning events. I believed in it – I still do. But belief doesn't prevent burnout.

I was also volunteering as a leader in Project Outreach, trying to be a good friend, a good student, and a good coworker. I wanted to do everything well. I wanted to be impressive, capable, kind, and helpful. I wanted to be the version of myself that people believed in.

But somewhere along the way, I started faking it. I smiled. I joked. I made it all look manageable. And maybe it was – on the surface. But inside, I was slipping. Even my friends could tell sometimes. I remember telling one of them just recently, "Sometimes it feels like you guys like me more than people at school do – because people at school just think I'm a workaholic glued to my Chromebook."

My days had become mechanical - school, nap, work, homework, sleep, repeat. I wasn't really living anymore. I was just managing. And then it cracked.

One night earlier this year, I started crying – hard – over the fact that I had, once again, woken up at 6:55 AM even though I needed forty minutes to get ready and had to leave by 7. It wasn't just about the situation. It was about everything. The rushing. The pressure. The constant sense that I was already behind.

I remember gripping my blanket and sitting in the dark, too wired to sleep, too tired to move. My chest felt tight, like I was running out of space inside myself. That was the night I told my parents I needed a therapist.

And I got one.

In the first few sessions, we talked through it all. The schedule. The expectations. The exhaustion. And we came to a hard truth: there wasn't anything I was doing that didn't matter. But I was the one getting lost in the middle of it.

A good comparison would be a burned batch of cookies - dark at the edges, stiff in the center, cracked where they should've been soft. Still cookies, technically. Still something good. But pushed too far. Left in too long.

I didn't literally burn a batch of cookies. But I didn't need to. I knew what they would've looked like – dark at the edges, stiff in the center, cracked where they should've been soft. Still cookies, technically. Still something good. But pushed too far. Left in too long.

That's what I felt like.

From the outside, I was doing everything right. I had the grades, the resumé, the leadership titles. I was holding it all together. But inside, I was drying out. The warmth that baking used to bring me – the comfort, the love – it had been replaced by pressure. Expectations. Exhaustion. I wasn't doing it for joy anymore. I was doing it to prove something.

I didn't literally burn a batch of cookies, but if I had, I think I would've stood there staring at them. Knowing I should've pulled them out sooner. But also knowing I was doing what I thought I had to. I don't have a perfect ending to this chapter. Things didn't magically get better. I didn't quit anything. I didn't slow down.

But I did start to notice how close I was to burning all the way through. It wasn't anyone else's oven this time – it was mine. And maybe that's where the change really begins: when you finally see the cracks along the edges and realize you're not supposed to stay in the heat forever.

Recipe: Chai Chocolate Chunk Cookies with Sea Salt

Why This Recipe

These cookies feel like that winter – oversized, crisp at the edges, and soft in the middle if you don't leave them in too long. I didn't actually burn a batch the night this story took place, but I didn't need to. I knew exactly what they would've looked like: dark around the outside, cracked through the center, technically whole, but pushed past the point of softness.

That's what I felt like then – something good, stretched thin, trying too hard to hold together. These cookies remind me of that moment. Of pressure mistaken for purpose. Of the warmth I used to bake for comfort, it became something I used to prove I was trying hard enough. The warmth and feelings that usually drove me when baking for comfort were instead replaced by the need to prove I was trying hard enough.

Now, when I make them, I take them out just before the edges go too far. I don't rush. I don't push. I let them be what they are – imperfect, sweet, still soft in the center. That feels like growth. That feels like me.

Ingredients

Cookie Dough

- 1 cup unsalted butter, browned and slightly cooled (226 g)
- 2 ¼ cups all-purpose flour (280 g)
- 1 tsp baking soda
- 1 tsp salt
- 2 tsp ground chai spice (or: 1 tsp cinnamon, ½ tsp cardamom, ¼ tsp ginger, ¼ tsp cloves)
- ¾ cup granulated sugar (150 g)
- ¾ cup packed brown sugar (165 g)
- 1 tsp vanilla extract
- 2 large eggs
- 2 cups chopped semi-sweet or dark chocolate chunks (350 g)
- Flaky sea salt, for topping

Directions

1. Brown the butter: In a saucepan over medium heat, melt butter until it foams, crackles, and turns golden brown with a nutty aroma (5-7 minutes). Let cool for 10-15 minutes.
2. In a medium bowl, whisk together flour, baking soda, salt, and chai spices.
3. In a large bowl, combine browned butter, both sugars, and vanilla. Mix until smooth.
4. Add eggs one at a time, beating well after each.
5. Slowly stir in the dry ingredients until just combined. Fold in chocolate chunks.
6. Cover and chill dough for at least 1 hour, preferably overnight.
7. Preheat the oven to 375°F (190 °C). Line baking sheets with parchment paper.
8. Scoop dough into rounded tablespoons and place on baking sheets, spaced apart.
9. Sprinkle tops with a pinch of flaky sea salt.
10. Bake for 11-13 minutes, slightly over-baking for golden brown edges and crisp tops.
11. Let cool on a baking sheet for 2 minutes, then transfer to wire racks.

Personal Note

I made these on February 6, 2025, and gave one to my older brother – big, warm, and just a little over-baked. It reminded me of something out of Willy Wonka – not perfect, but still full of magic.

Chapter 3: Skipping Meals

It didn't start with a decision.

It started with a feeling that who I was still wasn't enough.

Freshman year began with what should've felt like progress. I'd dropped from 190 pounds in middle school to around 155. People noticed. I did too – but not in the way you'd expect. Even with the weight gone, I still didn't like what I saw. It didn't feel like enough – not for me, and definitely not for who I wanted to be.

By spring, I joined the track team. I told myself it was for something new, something social – but honestly, it was also about shrinking. I thought maybe if I pushed hard enough, I could finally become someone people found attractive. And for someone like me – a gay teen figuring things out – it felt like being skinny was the only way to be seen that way. So I ran. I trained. I stopped eating.

Some days, I'd skip lunch altogether. Other days, I'd buy food just to throw it out before anyone noticed. At home, I served myself smaller portions at dinner and said I wasn't that hungry. But I was. I was starving most of the time. Still, hunger stopped feeling like a signal and started feeling like success.

I remember lying on the turf with my friend after school one day, the sun warming my face, everything quiet and still. It felt so good just to be there. Then our team captains shouted for us to get up and start warm-ups, and I just … couldn't. My body felt heavy, my mind foggy. I didn't want to move. I thought maybe I was just lazy – but really, I was running on nothing.

Sometimes I'd get dizzy when I stood up too fast. Other times, I'd zone out mid-conversation or forget what I was doing altogether. The world around me got fuzzier, but I convinced myself it was worth it. There wasn't logic. Just a rule: don't eat, and you'll get to where you want to be – wherever that even was.

When I started getting skinnier, people noticed that, too. "Why are you dieting? You're already skinny," they'd say. But it didn't matter. In my mind, I still wasn't enough.

My mom would ask what I'd eaten that day, and tell me I needed to eat more. Some days, that helped – like someone saw what I couldn't say out loud. Other days, it made me feel worse. Like I was doing something wrong by needing anything at all.

I've always loved food. I was to be a pastry chef. Food was supposed to be comfort – something warm, creative, safe. But when my body started to feel wrong, food started to feel wrong too. It didn't just feel off – it felt dangerous. Like one bite too many might undo everything.

There were nights I'd give in and eat too much, too fast, too desperately. I'd feel guilty and whisper to myself, "It's okay. I'll restart tomorrow." And in my head, that always meant midnight. Like I could erase everything with the ticking of a clock.

Eventually, not eating just became the new normal. I wasn't scared of hunger anymore. I was scared of what I meant if I stopped feeling it. Sometimes, I still think about that moment on the turf – how peaceful it felt to lie in the sun, and how impossible it felt to get back up. I didn't realize then that tiredness was a warning. I thought I just wasn't trying hard enough.

Everything from that time feels a little blurry now. I remember drinking Celsius instead of eating meals, grabbing candy or snacks, and forgetting when I last had something solid. Food stopped being a comfort. It just became something I couldn't get right.

I wasn't chasing control.

I was chasing enough.

It never started as a way to feel powerful. It started because I didn't like the way I looked – and I didn't think anyone else did either. I figured if I could just make my body look a certain way, I'd finally be seen. Noticed. Wanted.

The boys I found attractive all looked like that – Charlie from Heartstopper, Troye Sivan, Darren from Heartbreak High, and Timothée Chalamet. I didn't just want to be with them. I wanted to be them. I wanted their ease, their softness, the way they seemed to belong in their bodies. I thought if I looked like them, maybe I'd finally feel wanted, too.

So I stopped eating – not because I felt in control, but because I didn't feel like I had any other option. I thought maybe, if I skipped enough meals, I'd eventually wake up as someone better.

At the time, baking wasn't mine yet.

I hadn't discovered how much I'd come to love it – how it would become my safe space. My expression. My way back to myself. Back then, it was something I saw other people doing. Not something I believed belonged to me.

My days were a loop: school, track, homework, sleep. I didn't have a creative outlet. I didn't have a space to pour out what I was feeling. So I poured all of it – every ounce of pressure and self-doubt – into how little I could eat. How small I could become. How quiet I could stay.

I didn't know it then, but I wasn't just starving myself of food. I was starving myself of joy. Of softness. Of the very things that would one day help bring me back to life.

It cracked open slowly, quietly.

There wasn't a breakdown. Just a moment in the kitchen.

I was sitting at the table when my brother asked if I wanted something to eat. I shrugged. I didn't understand why he cared so much. But then he said more about food being fuel, about how I needed to eat to feel good. His voice was calm. Gentle. And for some reason, I listened.

That conversation didn't fix everything. But it cracked something open. I was tired. The rules I'd made to "fix" myself were the same ones keeping me stuck.

The real shift came when I started therapy. My therapist and I took an eating disorder assessment together. I didn't land in the clinical category. But I also didn't land in any other category. I was in the middle. And that space hurt. I wanted a name. A box. A reason. But what I had was real, even without the label.

No one really knew.

I didn't talk about it. I didn't think I could. And from the outside, I looked fine.

I used track to explain away the weight loss. I smiled in photos. I stayed involved. People said I looked great. Focused. Happy. And I smiled and nodded and carried the weight of being seen while feeling invisible.

Sometimes I wanted someone to see through it. But most of the time, I just wanted to be left alone to manage it. Shame kept me quiet. And in the quiet, I kept disappearing.

Eventually, I found the words.

Watching Heartstopper Season 2 was the first time I saw someone like me navigating something I hadn't known how to name. When Charlie's eating habits were brought up, it stuck. It felt too familiar.

Later, in therapy, the language came. My therapist explained that even if I wasn't "sick enough" by textbook standards, I was still struggling. Still hurting. Still valid. Learning the language gave me permission to stop minimizing it.

To start calling it what it was.

To begin again.

I'm not "cured". But I'm not where I was either.

Some days are still hard. That voice – the one that equates hunger with success – still shows up. But I don't let it lead anymore. I've stopped tracking calories. I've stopped punishing myself for being hungry. And when guilt creeps in, I reach for something small. Like a sausage, egg, and cheese on a croissant. Something warm. Something real.

Or ice cream – raspberry, in a waffle cone, with rainbow sprinkles. I had it recently, and it made me laugh out loud. It tasted like summer, even though it wasn't summer yet. It tasted like freedom.

There was a time when foods like that would've filled me with guilt. Now, I let them fill me with joy. Some days, I still struggle to love my body. But I'm learning I don't have to love it to feed it. I just have to respect it.

I think back to that day on the turf – how tired I was, how heavy everything felt. I didn't know it then, but that was the start of learning how to listen to my body instead of fighting it.

Maybe recovery isn't a finish line.

Maybe it's a quiet return to softness, to joy, to the version of myself I almost lost.

One meal at a time.

One moment at a time.

One bite at a time.

Recipe: Sausage, Egg, and Cheese Croissant Sandwich

Why This Recipe

For a long time, eating felt like something I had to earn. I measured worth in skipped meals, in empty stomachs, in how small I could make myself. Croissants felt indulgent. Breakfast sandwiches felt off-limits. But healing asks you to rewrite those rules.

This sandwich represents a shift, not just in how I eat, but in how I treat myself. It's warm, grounding, and layered with care. It reminds me that food isn't the enemy. It's a way back to joy, to presence, to the quiet decision to stay soft – even when it's hard.

Ingredients

Croissants

Dough (Day 1):

- 4 cups all-purpose flour (500 g)
- ¼ cup granulated sugar (50 g)
- 1 tbsp instant yeast (9 g)
- 2 tsp salt
- 1 ¼ cups warm milk (295 mL)
- 3 tbsp unsalted butter, melted (40 g)

Butter Block (Day 1):

- 1 cup unsalted butter, cold but pliable (225 g)

Egg Wash (Day 2):

- 1 egg
- 1 tbsp milk or water (15 mL)

The Good Stuff Inside

- Sausage patties (pork, turkey, or plant-based)
- Large eggs
- Slices of cheddar or American cheese
- 1 tbsp butter or oil (14 g) [for the eggs]
- Salt and pepper, to taste

Directions

For the Croissants

Day 1: Make the Dough & Butter Block

1. In a large bowl, whisk together flour, sugar, yeast, and salt. Add warm milk and melted butter. Mix until a shaggy dough forms. Knead for 3-4 minutes until smooth but not sticky. Wrap in plastic and chill for 30 minutes.
2. Make the butter block: Place the cold butter between two sheets of parchment paper. Pound and roll it out into a 7x7-inch square (about ½ inch thick). Keep it cold but pliable- like clay.
3. Laminate (First Fold): Roll your chilled dough into a 10x10-inch square. Place the butter block in the center like a diamond, then fold the corners of the dough over the butter to seal it like an envelope. Roll the dough into a 20x10-inch rectangle. Fold into thirds like a letter (this is your

first fold). Wrap and refrigerate for 30-45 minutes.

4. Repeat folds: Do two more rounds of rolling and folding (with 30-minute chills in between). After the third fold, wrap the dough tightly and refrigerate overnight.

Day 2: Shape and Bake

1. Roll and cut: On a floured surface, roll the dough into a large 20x10-inch triangle. Cut it in half lengthwise, then slice each half into four triangles (about 5 inches wide at the base) to make 8 croissants total.
2. Shape the croissants: Gently stretch each triangle, then roll from the base to the tip. Place them tip-side down on a parchment-lined tray. Curve into crescent shapes if you'd like.
3. Proof: Cover loosely and let rise in a warm place for 1 ½ to 2 hours, until puffy and jiggly.
4. Preheat oven to 375(190). Beat the egg with milk and brush lightly over croissants. Bake for 18-22 minutes, or until golden brown and flaky.
5. Cool completely on a wire rack before assembling the sandwiches.

To Assemble:

1. Preheat your oven to 350(175). Slice the croissants in half horizontally and place them on a baking sheet. Warm them in the oven for about 5 minutes while you prepare everything else.
2. In a skillet over medium heat, cook the sausage patties for about 3-4 minutes on each side, or until browned and fully cooked. Set aside and keep warm.
3. In the same skillet, melt butter on low heat. Crack in the eggs one egg at a time. You can scramble them softly or fry them sunny-side up — whatever feels right. Season with a bit of salt and pepper.

4. On each warm croissant, layer the sausage patty, egg, and a slice of cheese. If the cheese needs help melting, pop the whole sandwich (open-faced) back into the oven for a minute or two.

Personal Note

I first made this on March 16, 2024, using croissants we baked in bakeshop class. It was the first time I turned a class recipe into something of my own – and somehow, that made it taste even better.

Chapter 4: I Raised the Dough

I was sitting on my bed, wrapped in my green comforter, Grey's Anatomy playing in the background, when the thought landed – I need to do something good. Not for school. Not for a résumé. Just something that might actually help someone.

At the time, life felt repetitive. I went through the motions every day – class, homework, responsibilities – feeling busy but a little hollow. It wasn't sparked by any one moment – maybe just the quiet emptiness of another episode, another goodbye – but something in me shifted. I didn't want to keep coasting. I wanted to make a difference.

And I knew that it had to involve baking.

To me, food has always meant comfort. A warm cinnamon roll says what words sometimes can't – You're safe. You're seen. You're loved. Baking had always been a language of care, and I wanted to use it to reach others, especially those quietly struggling, like I was. I didn't have all the details yet, but I knew this would be about more than desserts. It would be about hope.

So I grabbed my Chromebook and started planning. I typed out menus and brainstormed names. I made a list of people to reach out to – teachers, friends, student leaders, even my sister's coworkers. I researched charities, mapped out a timeline, and began thinking of logistics. The fundraiser would run from February 5 to February 16. I'd bake. People would order. And somehow, all of it would matter.

At first, my parents weren't sure. They worried about the time, the cost, the outcome. But when I explained it – really explained it – they came around. They even offered to pay for the ingredients up front if I agreed to pay them back later. They believed in me. And suddenly, I started believing in me, too.

I remember sitting there that afternoon – Christmas tree still up at the end of my bed, my pet birds chirping in the corner, my room neatly organized like always. I was typing on my Chromebook, creating something from nothing. And for the first time in a long time, I didn't feel stuck. I felt ready.

At the time, my mental health was slowly getting better, but it was still messy. My eating was inconsistent, and I had days where sadness hung in the background like static. I was surrounded by supportive people, but I still felt like hiding. I wasn't being completely honest about what I was going through.

That's why this fundraiser meant so much to me. It gave me a way to do something. To take all the heaviness I was carrying and turn it into something sweet. Something soft. Something that might help someone else feel less alone.

When I found Mental Health Connecticut, I knew it was the right choice. They were based in my state, and I loved that their work wasn't about quick fixes. They were committed to long-term care, offering people not just help, but consistent support. They stayed. They checked in. They believed in recovery, not just treatment. That kind of commitment felt personal to me.

This bake sale wasn't just about fundraising. It was about using what I loved – baking – to support something I deeply believed in. And it felt different from anything I'd done before. It wasn't assigned. It wasn't expected. It was just mine. Something I was creating from scratch to make the world a little softer.

I was proud. And, to be honest, a little nervous. I wondered if people would question why I chose mental health. It wasn't Mental Health Awareness Month. What if they assumed I was struggling? What if it made me look weak? But the more I worked on it, the more I realized – this was me. All of me. And if people saw that, maybe that was a good thing.

My sister helped me price everything. I created a Google Form for pre-orders and regular orders. I ordered white boxes from Amazon, designed black-and-white labels on Canva, and printed stacks of them at Staples. I wanted everything to feel professional, thoughtful, and filled with care.

Not everything went smoothly. The cream puffs refused to cooperate at first.

I tried batch after batch, and none of them worked. There was one night when I almost gave up. I stood in the kitchen, exhausted and frustrated, watching another tray fall flat. But my mom helped me troubleshoot, and eventually we got it right.

It wasn't failure – it was a learning curve.

Balancing the fundraiser with school wasn't easy either. I'd go to class, rush home, finish homework, and bake until around 11:30 p.m. every night. For two weeks straight, every open moment was filled with mixing, shaping, folding, and labeling. But strangely, it didn't drain me. It energized me. I was doing what I loved. And I was doing it for people who needed to feel loved, too.

It was exhausting, yes. But it was the best kind of tired.

The atmosphere was nonstop.

At home, our kitchen turned into a two-lane highway – my parents trying to cook dinner while I rushed around finishing orders. At school, I'd email teachers asking when I could stop by. I started arriving early, around 6:45 a.m., to deliver boxes before the first channel. It was a lot to coordinate. But people worked with me. They cared.

And it showed. My friends, teachers, and even people I barely knew – so many supported the fundraiser. My sister's coworkers placed orders. Classmates shared the link. And the most unexpected part? Everyone was genuinely impressed. They commented on the taste, the portion sizes, the effort. It felt like people weren't just buying baked goods. They were investing in something I had built.

It lit me up inside. It reminded me that this dream – this passion – was more than just a hobby. It was a future. I wanted to feel that feeling forever. I still think about those late nights, baking while Zach Bryan played in the background. That specific blend of music, cinnamon, and purpose – it's something I wish I could bottle up and share with everyone.

One moment, that stuck, happened after the fundraiser ended. I was sitting at the kitchen table, calculator in hand, reviewing the number one last time. I double-checked everything, and there it was:

$500.

No confetti. No applause. Just a quiet, steady feeling that this mattered.

Then I typed up the message I'd send with the donation:

"My community and I are hopeful that individuals in CT facing mental health challenges will have an increase of resources and a brighter future. 💚"

I still think about that green heart. It wasn't just a symbol – it was a promise. A thank you. A quiet way of saying: This was real. And it meant something.

Looking back, it wasn't just a bake sale. It was a mirror. A beginning. A moment of becoming. I learned that it's okay to mess up. That baking, like life, doesn't ask for perfection – just care. Cream puffs collapse. Timers get missed. But showing up matters. Trying matters. Love matters.

In those long nights – flour on my sleeves, Zach Bryan in the background – I found something I hadn't felt in a while – clarity. I wasn't shrinking. I wasn't pretending. I was doing something meaningful. And I felt more like me than I had in a long time.

It changed how I saw my voice. I used to wonder if one person could really make a difference. But now I know they can even if that difference starts with a cinnamon roll and a label printed at Staples.

I don't just want to chase my goals anymore. I believe I can.

That fundraiser didn't just raise money – it raised belief. It reminded me that small actions, when done with heart, can ripple outwards in ways we never expect.

That was the first time I realized that baking could be more than comfort. It could be a connection. Advocacy. A way of saying: I see you. I care. You're not alone.

Someday, I want to open a bakery where people feel that same kind of warmth. A space where the cinnamon rolls are generous, the air smells like belonging, and no one leaves without feeling a little more okay. I will carry that dream with me to culinary school – where I'll keep learning, keep growing, and keep baking with purpose.

And I plan to keep baking that way – for people, and for myself – for a long, long time.

Recipe: Cinnamon Rolls

Why This Recipe

I made these cinnamon rolls during my first fundraiser for Mental Health Connecticut – a time when I needed to turn something heavy into something good. My mental health was still messy, but baking gave me a way to show up anyway.

Cinnamon rolls have always felt like a kind of care. They rise slowly, like healing. They're soft in the center, warm with cinnamon, and best when shared. These were made late at night, with flour on my sleeves and music in the background, and somehow they carried more than flavor. They carried hope.

This recipe reminds me that baking doesn't have to be perfect to mean something. It can be a way to speak without words. A way to say: You're seen. You're safe. You're loved.

Ingredients

Dough:

- ¾ cup warm whole milk (177 mL) [about 110]
- 2 ¼ tsp (1 packet) active dry yeast
- ¼ cup granulated sugar (50 g)
- 2 large eggs, room temperature
- ¼ cup unsalted butter, melted (60 g)
- 3 ¾ cups all-purpose flour, plus more for kneading (470 g)
- 1 tsp salt

Filling:

- ⅔ cup brown sugar, packed (140 g)
- 1 ½ tbsp ground cinnamon (11 g)
- ¼ cup unsalted butter, softened (60 g)

Cream Cheese Frosting

- 4 oz cream cheese, softened (115 g)
- ¼ cup unsalted butter, softened (60 g)
- 1 cup powdered sugar (120 g)
- ½ tsp vanilla extract
- Pinch of salt

Directions

For the Dough:

1. In a stand mixer bowl, combine warm milk and yeast. Let it sit for 5-10 minutes until foamy.
2. Add sugar, eggs, and melted butter. Mix until combined.
3. Add flour and salt. Mix with a dough hook on medium speed for 6-8 minutes until the dough is soft and slightly tacky.
4. Transfer to a greased bowl. Cover and let rise in a warm place for about 1 hour, or until doubled in size.

For the Filling:

1. In a small bowl, mix brown sugar and cinnamon. Set aside.
2. Roll out the dough on a floured surface to a 14x18-inch rectangle.
3. Spread the softened butter evenly over the dough. Sprinkle with the cinnamon sugar mixture.

To Roll and Bake:

1. Roll the dough tightly from the long edge to form a log. Slice into 6 equal pieces using dental floss or a sharp knife.
2. Arrange rolls in a greased 9x13-inch baking dish. Gently press down with your hand to flatten and create an even surface. Cover and let rise again for 30-45 minutes until puffy.
3. Preheat the oven to 350°F (175 °C). Bake the rolls for 20-25 minutes, or until golden brown and cooked through. Let cool slightly.

For the Frosting:

1. Beat cream cheese and butter until smooth. Add powdered sugar, vanilla, and salt. Mix until fluffy.
2. Spread the frosting onto warm rolls so that it melts into swirls.

Personal Note

I made these during the week of February 5-16, 2024, for my Mental Health Connecticut fundraiser. It was my first time baking for something bigger than myself.

Chapter 5: The Frosting Cracked

I created Wildcat's Voice with the hope it would play in the Community Meeting, the weekly space where our whole school came together for announcements, reminders, and moments that made us feel connected. That was the goal from the very beginning. It was April 2024 – just a few weeks before the end of the school year – and I didn't know if anyone would take it seriously, but I knew what it could mean if they did. I pictured students sitting in silence, just for a few minutes, hearing voices from people they knew, or didn't know, reminding them they weren't alone.

So I started piecing it together: shaky phone recordings, rushed one-takes filmed in busy hallways, quiet messages sent in late at night. One clip came in from a friend with an older Android, and the audio was rough. Another student sent theirs whispering in their bedroom, barely audible over the hum of a fan. I didn't ask anyone to re-record. I layered it all over a soft ambiance video of campus – trees moving, track field in the distance, the sun spilling across the pavement near Cranston (the Freshman building). It wasn't polished. But it was honest. And I believed in it enough to try.

The first voice you heard was mine.

"Hey Norwich Free Academy, sorry I missed you. This is us – the Wildcats. Within these messages, you'll hear your coworkers, friends, maybe just people you walk by every day, who've come together to create this video for you. Take this opportunity to breathe, recognize the words being said, and put your mental health first. This is ... Wildcat's Voice."

Recording that felt different than anything I'd done before. I had always cared – probably too much – about what people thought of me. About being respected. Seen the "right" way. But at that moment, I wasn't trying to impress anyone. I was just trying to say something honest. And somehow, that felt stronger than anything I'd ever done.

I came up with the idea during a season of quiet loneliness. I wasn't falling apart – I was still going to class, still working long hours. But I barely had time to be around people, let alone open up to them. I felt distant. Not because I didn't have people, but because I didn't have space to breathe.

Then, one night, I watched a video by a creator named Morgan Long. She had pieced together clips of strangers sharing encouragement – simple, real reminders to keep going. I didn't know any of them, and it still inspired me. I decided that something like that would really help me, but if it were from my peers, and if it could help me, it could probably help others, too.

The next morning, I told my sister.

"That's a great idea – if you can gain the support," she said.

That was all I needed. I reached out to the teacher who organized our school's community meetings. He said yes, but reminded me to walk the line carefully – that this wasn't a space for trauma dumping. That it had to be honest, but uplifting.

So I made a flyer. Posted it on Google Classrooms. Started asking everyone I could think of – friends, teachers, classmates I hadn't talked to in months to contribute. I worked on the video late at night after shifts, editing on Kinemaster in bed, headphones on, exhausted but alive at work. Every time someone submitted a clip, I lit up. But part of me was scared, too.

What if no one else joins in? What if this turns out ... disappointing?

Then the clips started to stack up. A student from a band. A teacher from the language department. My oldest brother, who had just started student teaching at NFA, sent in a message that made my breath catch: "We are more than the worst thing that we've ever done, or the worst place we've ever been in." Then he read a poem by Dr. Benjamin E. Mays.

Then our head of school submitted a clip of his own. That was when it hit me: This isn't just an idea anymore. This is real.

The night before it was scheduled to play, I stayed up late, rewatching the final cut. The audio wasn't perfect. The edits weren't flawless. But I was proud of what it stood for. Just as I was about to upload it, the file stalled. It wouldn't go through. I sat on my bed, refreshing again and again, silently begging the screen to work.

Eventually, it did.

The next morning, the lights dimmed in the classroom. We had just finished a long Global Studies in Citizenship class. Everyone knew this wasn't just another community meeting. The energy shifted. No one whispered. No one pulled out their phone. For 10 minutes, about 2,150 students and teachers sat in stillness – actually listening.

I didn't dare look around. My hands were sweaty. My stomach flipped. I kept thinking, I can't believe this is happening. And then ... silence.

Not the awkward kind. The real kind – the kind that holds something authentic and sacred.

Later that day, someone told me they had trouble hearing some of the audio. And they were right – it wasn't perfect. But by then, I knew it didn't have to be. The message had made it through.

That night, the email started.

A teacher I barely knew wrote, "Thank you. I cried watching it. I needed that today." Students messaged me. Some said it helped them feel less alone. One wrote, "This made me feel like I could breathe again – even if just for a little while. People actually understand what I'm going through." I read that one twice.

That night, I watched the video one last time – headphones in, lights off, back in my room. For the first time in weeks, I felt peaceful. Not because it was over, but because something about it felt complete.

And maybe for the first time, I didn't care what people thought of me. Not in a careless way. In a freeing way. Because this was the most honest thing I'd ever done. And if people didn't get it? That was okay. I wasn't here to convince them, I was here to create something good.

Wildcat's Voice started as a quiet idea in a tired moment. But it became something bigger than me. Something human. Something that reminded me of what leadership actually is. It's not about titles or spotlight. It's about creating space for others to feel seen.

This project wasn't flashy. It wasn't loud. It was vulnerable. It was real. And I think that's why it worked.

If I hadn't made this, I think I would've missed something huge. The sense of community it created – even if just for ten minutes – showed me what it means to bring people together through empathy, not authority. And now?

I want it to live on. That's why I've decided to pass it down to Ms. Harlow, the Project Outreach Coordinator who supported me through every step of this process. I know that even when I graduate – even when my name isn't attached to it – she'll find others to carry it forward. Because I want Wildcasts Voice to keep reminding people that their voice matters. That their story matters.

Someone said in one of the clips:

"The opposite of fear isn't bravery – it's faith and trust. And when anxiety takes us down the rabbit hole of imagining the worst, we forget we're not alone. You are never alone, not ever. So find someone or something to trust, and let that carry you through."

Another person said:

"I try to remind myself that most worries have an expiration date. Ask yourself – will this matter in a week, a month, a year? Probably not. So don't let it weigh you down today. Instead of borrowing trouble from tomorrow, reclaim some peace of mind."

I used to think leadership was about doing things that looked impressive. Now I know it's about creating something that feels like relief for someone else.

If someone watched this five years from now, I hope they feel like they can breathe again, even just for a little bit. And if I say something to the version of me on the floor, praying the upload would work? Little do you know – you're going to do it again next year. Even better. And it'll become something bigger than you ever imagined.

If you want to see it – the very first Wildcat's Voice – you still can. It's imperfect. Some clips are quiet. Some voices are shaky. But every second of it is real. It's not about production value. It's about honesty and the courage it takes to say, "You're not alone."

Watch here:
https://youtu.be/YP1UHZ92AJA?si=5KPfsKNeK2fm5bLW

Ten minutes. Many students' voices. A whole school of listening.

Recipe: Strawberry Shortcake with Only a Crumb Coat

Why This Recipe

I made this shortcake for the first time the summer after Wildcat's Voice. It wasn't meant to be symbolic – just something I baked on a quiet afternoon – but when I finished layering it, I couldn't stop thinking about that video.

It only had a crumb coat. You could still see the cake underneath, peaking out in all its unevenness. It didn't look polished. The strawberries were imperfectly placed, and the whipped frosting didn't smooth over the cracks. But it was full of softness. Full of care. And it tasted incredible. That's what Wildcats Voice was.

A patchwork of messages sent in shaky audio files. Clipped words. Background noise. Nothing about it is refined. But it was real – and that made it powerful. That made it matter.

This cake reminds me of the same truth:

You don't need a perfect finish to make something meaningful. You don't need to hide the layers to have an impact. Sometimes the most heartfelt things come through the clearest when you leave a few edges visible.

Ingredients

For the Cake Layers:

- Shortening or nonstick spray (for pans)
- All-purpose flour (for dusting pans)
- 1 cup salted butter, softened (227 g)
- 2 cups granulated sugar (400 g)
- 4 large eggs, separated
- 3 cups all-purpose flour (360 g)
- ¼ tsp salt
- 1 cup milk (240 mL)
- 1 tbsp baking powder (12 g)
- ¼ tsp vanilla extract

- ½ tsp almond extract
- 2 pints fresh strawberries (900 g)

Dreamy Whipped Frosting:

- 8 oz mascarpone cheese, softened (225 g)
- ⅔ cup granulated sugar, divided (133 g)
- 2 cups heavy whipping cream (473 mL)
- ½ tsp vanilla extract
- ½ tsp almond extract

Directions

1. Preheat oven to 350 (175). Grease two 9-inch round cake pans with shortening or nonstick spray and dust with flour.
2. In a large bowl, beat the softened butter until fluffy. Gradually add in the sugar, beating well. Add the egg yolks one at a time, mixing just until combined.
3. In a separate bowl, whisk together flour, baking powder, and salt.
4. Add to the butter mixture in three parts, alternating with milk, beginning and ending with dry ingredients.
5. Stir in vanilla and almond extracts.
6. In a clean bowl, beat the egg whites until stiff peaks form. Gently fold one-third of the whites into the batter, then fold in the rest in two more additions.
7. Divide the batter evenly between pans. Bake for 28-32 minutes or until a toothpick inserted in the center comes out clean. Let cool in pans for 10 minutes, then transfer to a wire rack to cool completely (about 1 hour).
8. Hull and slice about 20-25 strawberries into even ¼-inch thick slices. Set aside for layering.

9. Make the whipped frosting: In a bowl, stir together the mascarpone cheese and half of the sugar. In another bowl, beat the heavy cream, vanilla, and almond extract until foamy. Slowly add the remaining sugar and beat until stiff peaks form. Fold one-third of the whipped cream into the mascarpone mixture to lighten it, then fold in the rest gently.

10. Assemble the cake: Place one cake layer on a platter. Spread about ¾ cup frosting evenly on top. Arrange a layer of sliced strawberries over the frosting, overlapping slightly. Spread a thin layer of frosting over the strawberries to cover them. Repeat with another layer of sliced strawberries and another thin layer of frosting, creating 2-3 layers of strawberries total.

11. Add the second layer of cake on top. Spread the remaining frosting over the top and sides. Garnish with slices and whole strawberries if desired.

12. Chill before slicing for best texture – although it's just as good, slightly messy, and served with a fork fresh from the fridge.

Personal Note

I made this on August 9, 2024, during a quiet summer afternoon when I finally had time to try cake decorating. It wasn't perfect – the layers leaned, and frosting barely covered the sides – but it still felt worth sharing. The kind of cake you'd give someone just to say, hey, it's okay not to have it all together.

Chapter 6: Kneaded by Friends

It wasn't one night. It wasn't one sleepover or conversation or single moment that made it click. It was a hundred little ones – quiet, chaotic, and full of laughter – that slowly stitched themselves into something that felt like home. Summer's room became a kind of landing place. Not perfect, not polished, but warm. There were always too many shoes by the door, music playing from her phone speaker, and us – just us – talking like time didn't exist.

That's when I met Tina, actually at Summer's birthday party. We ended up near the couch, batting balloons back and forth across the floor like cats, chasing them for no reason other than it made us laugh. At one point, we cut one open and talked in helium voices until we were gasping for air between laughs. I didn't know it then, but that was the beginning of the best friendship I didn't even know I was missing.

That kind of ridiculousness defined us and was somehow present every time we were together. Tina and I walked into a Mattress Firm pretending to be a British couple from Queens. We asked the employee, with straight faces and the worst accents ever, what mattress would be best for our guest bedroom back home. She led us through the store like it was the most normal thing in the world, and somehow we never broke character. We still don't know how we pulled it off.

Then there was the time we needed fresh air at a party and came back dragging a random chair we found on the side of the road, giggling like idiots the whole way. I'm still convinced that chair had haunted energy, but we brought it back anyway.

Or when we snuck out for a late-night Walgreens run while Summer slept, picked up peanut M&Ms, and split garlic knots from a pizza place where the guy tossed in an extra one, just because.

And then there was Boston.

That whole day felt like a movie – walking down Newbury Street, shopping way more than we should've, stopping at this little photo booth place where we took pictures we'll probably laugh at forever. We ate so much good food. It was cold, but we didn't care. It felt like freedom. Like joy. Like being fully known by someone who doesn't just see you, but chooses to go through life next to you.

And there was Senior Sunset.

We sat in the grass playing giant Uno while the sky hovered above us, the cloudiest it could probably be. No glowing sunset, no golden light. Just us, laughing away. After Tina left, Summer realized she'd locked her keys in the car. So we climbed onto the hood and just lay there, talking about everything and nothing while we waited for someone to unlock it. The NFA parking lot was nearly empty, but for some reason, it felt like the center of the universe.

There were quieter moments too. Lying on the couch at Mohegan Sun one night, half-asleep and doing absolutely nothing, but feeling completely at peace. Or the three of us lying in Summer's car, where it was somehow always warm, almost like a sauna. It was quiet, calm, and weirdly peaceful, like we could've stayed there forever.

And there were wild, joyful moments – like the day Summer and I went to the beach, and Tina came by later. The water was freezing, the kind of cold that burns your legs when you run through it. But Tina and I jumped in anyway, screaming, splashing like it was the middle of summer. Summer just sat on the towel laughing, shaking her head. It was chaos. It was perfect.

What I found in Tina and Summer wasn't just friendship. It was a kind of permission to be myself without overthinking it. To be silly, serious, sarcastic, soft. To say the weird things I was thinking without worrying how they'd sound. Around them, I didn't feel the need to prove anything or be perfect. Even getting ready together – putting on makeup or doing our hair side-by-side – felt easy. No judgement. No pressure. Just comfort in being completely real.

They were the first people I let see parts of myself I usually keep tucked away. The parts that liked dressing up just because. The parts felt a little softer than I was used to. The parts I wasn't always sure the world was ready for – but they were.

Summer taught me that things aren't always going to work out, and we're not always going to agree. We've had our moments – I'm friends with her ex, and that wasn't easy for either of us. But I think the biggest thing I've learned from her is this: if someone truly matters to you, you have to trust they'll know even if things get complicated, even if it's messy. You have to believe the love you show them will speak louder than anything else.

Tina brings out the spontaneous in me. Being around her makes everything feel lighter, more open, like I'm allowed to just say yes to whatever moment we're in. She reminds me what it feels like to dive in – literally, sometimes – and laugh until I forget what I was worried about in the first place.

When I started high school, I wasn't sure I'd ever click with anyone this deeply. I spent most of middle school floating, half-included, but never quite seen. I didn't think friendships like this existed for people like me.

I don't think I truly realized how much they both mean to me until this year. Somewhere between dancing with Tina for two hours straight at junior prom, and all the times I FaceTimed Summer just because I needed someone, and she always picked up, somewhere between the absurd, the soft, and the completely ordinary.

And then graduation happened.

I wasn't even graduating – I was volunteering as an usher, wearing a red sash and standing off to the side. But I was in the crowd, screaming their names when they walked across the stage. And that's when it hit me that they were really leaving. That this part of our lives was actually ending. My eyes welled up, and I just let it happen. I cried – not because I wasn't going to be okay, but because I already missed the feeling of being around them.

For a little while, if I'm being honest, I was angry. Not at them – but at the whole idea of it. That they got to move on while I stayed behind. That they were stepping into the next version of their lives, and I was still here, standing exactly where they stood a year ago. It made me feel stuck. Small. Like I was being left in a space that didn't quite fit anymore.

But even through that, I knew something else was true, too.

Before them, I didn't know friendship could feel like this. I didn't know how deeply someone could know you without needing to fix you. How real love doesn't ask you to shrink or change – it just holds you where you are, messy and honest and entirely enough.

And honestly? I've never had so much fun as I have had with them. Not even close. With Tina, everything feels YUMMY- her word, not mine, but somehow exactly right. And Summer? She feels safe. She feels true. When I'm with them, it's like the world shrinks down to just us. Like all the heaviness from the earlier chapters – the things I've carried quietly – slip through the cracks for a while. Like I can finally breathe.

If they're ever reading this: thank you. Thank you for showing me what real love looks like. I hope to find that kind of friendship in others someday. I want to help people feel the way you helped me feel – like being yourself is more than enough. And I hope I'll see you again, even if only once in a blue moon.

My younger self would probably look at me now and wonder what happened. I used to be so stressed out, so uptight, always trying to do things right. But somehow, you taught me how to laugh louder. How to show up as myself. How to actually have fun.

Please don't forget about me. I'll miss you more than I can say.

Recipe: Chocolate Babka Bread

Why This Recipe

Babka is braided and imperfect – a little chaotic, a little sweet – but beautiful because of it. Every twist in the dough reminds me of friendship at its best: messy, real, and full of joy. You have to get your hands in it, shape it with care, and trust that it will rise into something soft and golden.

This recipe feels like Tina and Summer. Like spontaneous adventures and the kind of laughter that bubbles up without warning. Like laughing until we can't breathe, then sitting in stillness, knowing we didn't have to say a word. It's a reminder that the best things aren't always neat or expected – they're layered, warm, and meant to be shared. Babka holds everything all at once, just like we did.

Ingredients

Dough

- 4 ½ cups all-purpose flour (540 g)
- ½ cup granulated sugar (100 g)
- 2 ¼ tsp instant yeast (1 packet)
- 4 large eggs, room temperature
- ½ cup whole milk, room temperature (120 mL)
- 1 ½ tsp kosher salt
- 10 tbsp unsalted butter, room temperature (142 g)

Filling

- ½ cup unsalted butter, cubed (113 g)
- ½ cup heavy cream (120 mL)
- 8 ounces dark chocolate, chopped (225 g)
- ¾ cup powdered sugar (90 g)
- ⅓ cup unsweetened cocoa powder (30 g)

For the Syrup

- ⅓ cup granulated sugar (66 g)
- ⅓ cup water (80 mL)

Directions

For the Dough

1. In the bowl of a stand mixer, whisk together the flour, sugar, and yeast.
2. Add the eggs, milk, and salt. Mix with the dough hook on low until a rough dough forms, about 2 minutes.
3. Add the butter a tablespoon at a time, letting it blend fully before adding more.
4. Once all the butter is in, keep kneading for about 10 minutes until it's stretchy and elastic. It will feel sticky but strong.
5. Transfer to a large, oiled bowl. Cover and refrigerate overnight (or at least 8 hours).

For the Filling

1. In a small saucepan, heat butter and cream over medium heat until melted and steaming.
2. Add the chopped chocolate and stir until smooth.
3. Remove from heat, whisk in the powdered sugar and cocoa powder.
4. Let cool on the counter until it's cool to the touch, then transfer to the refrigerator and chill until it thickens into a spreadable consistency.

To Assemble

1. Butter and line two 8x4-inch loaf pans.
2. On a floured surface, divide the dough in half. Keep one half chilled while working with the other.
3. Roll into a 12x16-inch rectangle. Spread on half the filling, leaving a 1-inch border on one short edge.
4. Roll tightly from the opposite short side. Pinch the seam closed.
5. Slice the roll lengthwise. Twist the halves together with cut sides facing up – messy but intentional.
6. Place into a prepared loaf pan. Repeat with the remaining dough and filling.
7. Cover and let rise in a warm place until puffy, about 1 ½-2 hours.
8. Preheat the oven to 350 (175).
9. Bake for 40 minutes, until golden and a toothpick comes out clean.
10. While baking, simmer sugar and water until dissolved.
11. Brush loaves with syrup as soon as they come out of the oven.
12. Let cool for 30 minutes.

Personal Note

I made this babka bread on February 23, 2024, during my Bakeshop 2 class. It was one of the first recipes that taught me to embrace the mess – to twist something imperfect into something beautiful. It reminded me a lot of friendship: layered, warm, and better when shared.

Chapter 7: Let It Rest

It was sometime in the middle of junior year, though I couldn't have told you exactly when. Most days blurred together – early alarms, late shifts, another homework assignment, another club meeting, another customer asking where the fitting room was. I wasn't falling apart, but I wasn't fully there either.

I wasn't trying to be dramatic. I was just doing what I had to do. The Connecticut Association of Student Councils (CASC) mattered to me — it was a chance to lead, to create change, and to do something that actually felt meaningful. And yeah, it didn't hurt that it looked good on a resume, too. Honors classes were for college. TJ Maxx was for savings, and for the little things I wanted to buy. Even my therapist agreed: none of it was pointless. Everything had a reason.

Still, I was always tired. The kind of tiredness that gets into your bones and settles there. I'd leave work at 10, grab food on the way home, and finish my homework in bed while my eyes burned. Then I'd be up at 6, doing it all again. Sometimes I felt like a machine that only worked when there was something to do.

I stopped sitting with my friends during free moments. Not out of spite – just because I had things to finish. I was always on my Chromebook: at lunch, in the hallway, in the back of other classes when I wasn't caught up. There was always something else to turn in, something else to check off the list. If I could finish now, maybe I'd sleep a little more later.

People started noticing – not in dramatic ways, just little comments. In Spanish class, I'd be working on everything except Spanish. Someone would glance over and say, "You're always doing something." And I'd just shrug. It didn't feel optional. It felt necessary.

The one place that felt different was Brickview – our school's student-run bakeshop class. We ran it like a restaurant: prepping, plating, serving, and cleaning up after ourselves. But it never felt like pressure. There was flour in the air and laughter over the sinks. I'd lose track of time folding croissant dough or watching cakes rise.

That kitchen felt like a bubble. Like nothing could go wrong. Some days, I'd be elbow-deep in butter and sugar, and everything else just fell away. I wasn't worrying about my transcript. I wasn't checking the clock. I was just ... present. And that was rare.

It wasn't a break from my goals – it was the goal. That's what I wanted to do. And even on the hardest days, it reminded me.

Eventually, I started realizing I wanted more of that feeling.

TJ Maxx taught me a lot, and I don't regret working there. But I'm 17, pulling supervisor-level duties, and still making barely above minimum wage. It was starting to feel like I was giving too much to something that couldn't give back.

So I started talking to people – coworkers, friends, and Ms. Ellis, my Honors Public Speaking teacher. She always pushed us to speak the truth, to ask what we actually wanted. I trusted her. I started listening to myself.

When I finally gave my notice at TJ Maxx, I cried. I'd been there so long. I'd grown close with my coworkers, and closing that final night came with hugs from everyone. It wasn't dramatic – just quiet and sad. Like the end of a chapter, I wasn't quite ready to leave, but knew I had to.

Still, I was ready for something new.

I found a job in food service – a calmer environment, slower pace. The dining room was peaceful, the kind of place where people said "thank you" and meant it. Everyone seemed kind. I got out by 7. I had time to eat dinner, catch up on homework, and maybe even text a friend without my brain spiraling about deadlines.

On my first shift, I remember standing behind my trainer, a little nervous, watching the way the residents smiled when their plates arrived. It was simple.

It was warm. And for the first time in a while, I wasn't faking calm – I actually felt it.

It was a shift I didn't even realize I needed. And for the first time in a long time, I looked forward to going to work. I didn't have to brace myself before every shift. I wasn't counting the hours until it ended. I could breathe.

On weekdays, I worked in the dining room. And on weekends, I started a second job at a family-owned bakery – a place that smelled like fresh bread and warm sugar the moment you walked in. The shelves were filled with every type of baked good you could imagine. Just the kind of place I'd always dreamed of working in someday. I ran the front counter on Saturdays and Sundays, helping each customer find something sweet to take home.

Between the slower evenings, the stillness of the bakeshop, and not having to micromanage every assignment, something inside me softened. I wasn't coasting, but I wasn't running myself dry either. And maybe that's the biggest thing I've learned: it's OK to take a breather. The world doesn't fall apart when you rest. You don't fall apart either.

Everything is going to be ok, even if you let yourself pause.

I didn't stop everything. I just let some parts rest – the ones that needed it most.

Recipe: Cookie Croissants

Why This Recipe

Cookie croissants are buttery, rich, and a little bit indulgent – like taking time you didn't think you could spare. They're slow by design. You can't rush the layers or skip the resting time. And they remind me of when I finally let myself pause.

I used to think working nonstop was the only way to feel accomplished. But leaving the job that drained me and finding ones that felt right – jobs that made space for breathing – showed me something different.

These croissants taught me that rest isn't wasted time. It's what helps everything come together in the end.

Ingredients

Croissants

Dough (Day 1):

- 4 cups all-purpose flour (500 g)
- ¼ cup granulated sugar (50 g)
- 1 tbsp instant yeast
- 2 tsp salt
- 1 ¼ cups warm milk
- 3 tbsp unsalted butter, melted (40 g)

Butter Block (Day 1):

- 1 cup unsalted butter, cold but pliable (225 g)

Egg Wash (Day 2):

- 1 egg
- 1 tbsp milk or water

Cookie Dough Filling

- 12 tbsp unsalted butter, softened (170 g)
- ⅔ cup brown sugar (130 g)
- ½ cup granulated sugar (100 g)
- 1 tsp vanilla extract
- 1 tsp salt
- 1 ½ cups semi-sweet chocolate chips (180 g)
- 1 cup all-purpose flour (120 g)

Topping (optional):

- Flaky salt
- Extra chocolate chips

Directions

For the Croissants

Day 1: Make the Dough & Butter Block

1. In a large bowl, whisk together flour, sugar, yeast, and salt. Add warm milk and melted butter. Mix until a shaggy dough forms. Knead for 3-4 minutes until smooth but not sticky. Wrap in plastic and chill for 30

minutes.

2. Make the butter block: Place the cold butter between two sheets of parchment paper. Pound and roll it out into a 7x7-inch square (about ½ inch thick). Keep it cold but pliable - like clay.

3. Laminate (First Fold): Roll your chilled dough into a 10x10-inch square. Place the butter block in the center like a diamond, then fold the corners of the dough over the butter to seal it like an envelope. Roll the dough into a 20x10-inch rectangle. Fold into thirds like a letter (this is your first fold). Wrap and refrigerate for 30-45 minutes.

4. Repeat folds: Do two more rounds of rolling and folding (with 30-minute chills in between). After the third fold, wrap the dough tightly and refrigerate overnight.

Day 2: Shape and Bake

1. Roll and cut: On a floured surface, roll the dough into a large 20x10-inch rectangle. Cut it in half lengthwise, then slice each half into six triangles (about 4 inches wide at the base) to make 12 croissants total.

2. Shape the croissants: Gently stretch each triangle, then roll from the base to the tip. Place them tip-side down on a parchment-lined tray. Curve into crescent shapes if you'd like.

3. Proof: Cover loosely and let rise in a warm place for 1 ½ to 2 hours, until puffy and jiggly.

4. Preheat oven to 375 (190). Beat the egg with milk and brush lightly over croissants. Bake for 18-22 minutes, or until golden brown and flaky.

5. Cool completely on a wire rack before assembling the cookie croissants.

While They Cool: Make the Cookie Dough

1. In a medium bowl, cream together softened butter, brown sugar, and granulated sugar.

2. Add vanilla and salt, then mix in flour until just combined.
3. Fold in mini chocolate chips.

To Assemble

1. Cut each cooled croissant in half horizontally.
2. Scoop 1-2 tablespoons of cookie dough onto the bottom half.
3. Place the top half back on like a sandwich.
4. Return to a parchment-lined baking sheet and bake again at 350(175) for 15-18 minutes, or until the cookie dough is baked through while still slightly gooey in the center.

Personal Note

I made these on January 29, 2025, using croissants I had baked at home. I stuffed them with warm cookie dough on a whim – and somehow, it turned into something entirely my own. Rich, messy, and kind of magical.

Chapter 8: Still Rising

It's a weird feeling – writing a book at seventeen. I'm sitting criss-cross applesauce on my bed, my lamp casting a soft glow across the room. Conan Gray's The Story plays softly in the background, the words "it's not the end of the story" settling into the quiet like a promise. It's late, but I'm not rushing. I'm not stressing. I'm just here. Still rising.

Most nights look like this lately – me, in the quiet, writing. After a long day of working, hanging out with friends, and showering, this is how I unwind. Some chapters came out of me like breath. Others took longer - they were tighter, heavier. But all of them brought me a little closer to something that felt like peace.

This summer has moved fast. My mornings are slow – I wake up, talk with friends, and we sit around until someone suggests a plan. By afternoon, I'm getting ready for work. On weekdays, I head to the dining room, where my shift starts at four and ends at seven. On weekends, I work at the bakery, helping customers find fresh bread and pastries. I don't leave drained like I used to. That's part of why I changed jobs – to stop feeling burnt out all the time. Now, when I come home, I still have energy left to actually enjoy the rest of my life.

Senior year is two months away. I'm writing a memoir. My dad's editing it. My sister is designing the covers. This thing that started as a quiet idea is becoming something real. And college? It's coming, too. But I'm not overwhelmed like I was in junior year. I'm just curious. Excited. There are so many directions life could go – maybe a gap year, maybe community college, maybe Johnson &

Wales, my dream school. Or maybe something else entirely. I don't need the answer right now. For the first time, I'm okay taking it day by day.

This summer hasn't been flashy – it's been full of small, good things. One day, Tina, Hunter, and I went hiking and found a waterfall. We hadn't brought towels or planned for anything. But when we saw it, we jumped in. The kind of cold that takes your breath away, the kind of laughter that echoes. Another night, we went to the drive-in – me, Tina, her sister, and a friend. We brought snacks, bug spray, and blankets. I remember sitting on the roof of the car, the movie glowing in the distance, and all of us falling quiet. Not because we were bored, but because the sky was soft and the moment was full.

Then there was a night in Summer's car. Just me, Tina, and Summer. We talked about the future – college, moving on, and missing each other. I told them I want to be a pastry chef, but that I'm not trying to control everything anymore. I'll go where life takes me. We were all close to tears, and for some reason, we started touching each other's knees. We called it a "knee connection." It made no sense, but it made us laugh. It made us feel close.

Not everything was emotional. One night, I decorated my car – the one I got from my great-grandmother, Nanny. It didn't take long. I hung a lavender Labubu from the dashboard, tucked a blanket and some pillows in the back, and picked a scent for the air vent that reminded me of summer. My dad and I took it for a drive down the winding road near our house, Zach Bryan playing through the speakers. Neither of us said much. We didn't need to.

Later this summer, my dad and I are going to visit Saint Michael's College, where I was nominated for a book award. We've been planning it for weeks, and I've been counting down. Just being on campus, walking around, and imagining what the future might hold — I can't wait.

Writing this book has helped me breathe. Really breathe. I was afraid when I started. Afraid of being judged, afraid that no one would understand, afraid it wouldn't matter. I still don't know if it'll ever be published. But I hope it is. Because if it helps even one person feel less alone, that's enough.

Since chapter one, a lot has changed.

My relationship with my parents, especially my mom, has grown in ways I never expected. She's been incredible – supportive, steady, loving. Even when we don't agree on everything, she still shows up. There was a time I felt like I had to hide parts of myself to keep the peace, like being fully me would be too much. But now, I'm completely out. I feel more seen, safe, and wanted than I used to, and my mom knows. She still loves me. She's still here. That means more than I can say.

My relationship with food changed, too, in quiet, steady ways. It isn't something I overthink every minute of the day. It doesn't feel like a test I'm always failing. Most of the time, it's just food – and that feels like a small miracle. Some days, the old thoughts still show up, but they don't run my life anymore. I'm learning to meet myself with patience, even when it's hard. To keep showing up for my body, whether or not I feel like I deserve it. I'm learning that progress isn't loud or perfect – it's a series of ordinary moments where I choose care instead of criticism.

I'm not exhausted the way I used to be. Leaving what wasn't working was hard, but it opened space for something gentler. Now, when the day ends, I still have something left to give – to myself, to the people I care about. I still get tired, but it's the kind that feels natural, not the kind that empties me out.

Most of all, I'm learning how to be here. To stop measuring my worth by how exhausted I am or how much I can juggle. To let go of perfection. To rest. To just exist. I've learned that slowing down doesn't mean giving up. It means making space for something better to grow.

And I didn't do it alone. Organizing Mental Health Connecticut fundraisers, building Wildcats Voice from the ground up, standing beside friends who feel like family – that's what carried me forward. That's what reminded me, over and over, that I'm allowed to take up space. I'm allowed to take a breath.

I'm starting to feel ok in my own skin. Not perfect. Not always. But more ok than I ever thought I could be. And maybe that's enough. Maybe that's everything.

A few days ago, I went to Six Flags. I got on the swings – the ones that lift you up so high you can see the whole park. The wind was wild. My legs dangled. Everything looked small from up there. For a few moments, everything felt still. The stress, the plans, the next steps – they all went quiet. I didn't think about where I was going. I just let myself rise.

Sometimes I think about the version of me who lived out chapter one. The boy who felt small and scared and unsure of everything. I think he'd be relieved to see where we are now. Relieved to know that the worst parts didn't last forever. Those things really did get better. Not perfect – but real. And hopeful. And full of love.

And if I ever forget – if I ever find myself buried in the stress of rushing through life again – I hope I remember this summer. I hope I remember what I've learned over these past three years: that it's ok to slow down. That I don't have to have all the answers. That just being here, becoming, rising – that's enough.

This whole book – *Three Years of Learning to Be Enough* – has led me here. And I'm still rising. And maybe, just maybe – that's enough.

Recipe: No-Knead Dutch Oven Bread

Why This Recipe

This bread doesn't need to be kneaded or rushed. You mix the dough, cover it, and wait. It rises slowly, on its own time, without pressure, without perfection, and somehow, that's enough.

That's what this chapter feels like: letting go of control, learning to breathe, and trusting that quiet progress still counts. This summer isn't loud or dramatic – it is full of soft moments that add up to something meaningful.

This recipe reminds me of that kind of growth. The kind that takes its time. The kind you don't always notice while it's happening. The crust turns golden. The center stays soft. And when it's ready, it fills the room with warmth.

It's steady. It's simple. And it's proof that sometimes, becoming doesn't have to be hard. Sometimes, you just need to give yourself the time to rise.

Ingredients

Dough

- 3 ½ cups all-purpose flour (450 g)
- 2 tsp salt
- ½ tsp instant yeast
- 1 ⅓-1 ½ cups warm water (340-350 mL)
- Optional: cornmeal or flour, for dusting

Directions

1. In a large bowl, stir together the flour, salt, and yeast. Gradually add the warm water, mixing until a shaggy dough forms. The dough should feel slightly sticky but not soupy. If it seems too wet to hold a loose shape, sprinkle in 1-2 tablespoons of flour at a time until it comes together.

2. Cover the bowl tightly with plastic wrap or a clean, dry towel. Let it rest at room temperature for 12-18 hours, until the surface is bubbly and the dough has doubled in size.

3. Lightly flour a work surface. Gently turn the dough out and fold it in from the edges toward the center 5-6 times to build tension. Flip it over, smooth side up, and cup your hands around it, gently pulling toward you to form a tighter ball. Let it rest for 15 minutes.

4. Shape it into a round ball and place it seam-side down on a piece of parchment paper (dust with flour or cornmeal if sticky. Cover loosely with a dry kitchen towel and let it rise for 1-2 hours, until puffy and slightly larger.

5. Meanwhile, preheat your oven to 450 (230) with a Dutch oven inside (lid on) for at least 30 minutes.

6. When the dough is ready, carefully remove the Dutch oven from the oven. Use the parchment paper to lift the dough and gently place it inside. Cover with the lid and bake for 30 minutes.

7. Remove the lid and bake uncovered for another 10-15 minutes, until the crust is deep golden and crisp.

8. Lift the bread out using the parchment and let it cool on a wire rack before slicing.

Personal Note

I made this bread during the summer of 2025, when life finally felt a little slower. It didn't take much – just flour, water, time, and trust. But watching it rise reminded me that good things don't have to be complicated. Sometimes, the simplest things bring the most comfort.

Acknowledgments

This book wouldn't exist without the people who reminded me – gently, consistently – that my story was worth telling.

To my family: thank you for being part of this with me. Dad, thank you for your patience, your encouragement, and for helping me shape these words into something real. Mom, thank you for how far we've come. Your steady support means more than I can say. To my sister B, thank you for bringing the original cover to life and always cheering me on. To Sis and Geoff, thank you for giving me reasons to laugh and chances to forget about everything else for a while. And to Phoenix and Kempton – thanks for being there, even when we drive each other a little crazy. I'm glad we got to grow up together.

To my teachers: Ms. Coronado, thank you for helping me find my voice when I didn't always believe it mattered. Mrs. Gada, thank you for seeing me in the quiet moments and always rooting for my growth. Mrs. Dooley, thank you for reminding me that being a leader doesn't always mean having it all figured out — it just means caring enough to keep showing up. Mrs. Reed and Mrs. Szczygiel – thank you for creating a classroom that felt like home and for showing me how healing baking can be. Each of you has shaped more than just these pages – you've shaped the person writing them.

To Randi, thank you for designing the new cover. I really appreciate the time and care you put into it.

To my closest friends, Rosie and Nora – thank you for the memories, the softness, the chaos, the calm. You showed up for me in a thousand small ways, and those moments became the heart of this book.

And to you, the person holding this book, thank you. Whether you've read every page or just a few, I hope you carry this reminder with you: you don't have to be perfect to be worthy. You're already enough.

Resources

If you connected with any part of this book and you're looking for support, guidance, or someone to talk to, please know this: you're not alone. Below are organizations and communities that offer help, healing, and hope.

Mental Health Support

- **988 Suicide & Crisis Lifeline**

Call or text **988** | 988lifeline.org
   Free, confidential support is available 24/7 for anyone in emotional distress or supporting someone else.

- **Crisis Text Line**

Text **HOME** to **741741** | crisistextline.org
   Connect with trained crisis counselors anytime via text.

- **Mental Health Connecticut** | mhconn.org

A statewide organization focused on mental health wellness, advocacy, and recovery.

Eating Disorder Support

· **National Eating Disorders Association (NEDA)**

1-800-931-2237 | nationaleatingdisorders.org
Offers resources, screening tools, and a helpline for those struggling with eating disorders and body image.

· **Project HEAL**

theprojectheal.org
Provides financial support and case management support to make eating disorder treatment accessible, especially for underserved communities.

· **ANAD (National Association of Anorexia Nervosa and Associated Disorders)**

anad.org
Free peer support groups, mentorship, and recovery resources for all eating disorders.

LGBTQ+ Support

· **The Trevor Project**

1-877-488-7386 | Text **START** to **678-678** | thetrevorproject.org
Crisis intervention and suicide prevention for LGBTQ+ youth.

· **It Gets Better Project**

itgetsbetter.org
A global movement sharing uplifting stories and resources for LGBTQ+ youth and allies.

Creative Coping Through Baking

Sometimes healing begins in small, sweet ways. Baking has been one of my hobbies. Whether you're mixing dough at midnight or just flipping through recipes for comfort, let it be something gentle. You don't have to be perfect to create something good. You're allowed to mess up, to try again, and to find joy in the process.

Please Remember

You are not a burden. You are not broken.
    You are worthy of rest, softness, support, and love, just as you are.
    Healing isn't linear. Some days are hard, but you are still here.
    And that is enough.
    With love,
    Kinnick

About the Author

Kinnick Campbell is a small-town baker, student leader, yoga instructor, and mental health advocate from Connecticut. He began writing *Three Years of Learning to Be Enough: One Day, One Recipe* at seventeen, blending personal stories with symbolic recipes to capture three years of growth, healing, and learning to be enough.

Throughout high school, Kinnick raised over $3,000 for Mental Health Connecticut through bake sales, served as President of the Connecticut Association of Student Councils, and created Wildcat's Voice – a mental health video initiative designed to help students feel less alone. His work centers around storytelling, connection, and creating spaces where people feel seen, supported, and safe.

Kinnick will study business in college and hopes to one day run a restaurant, café, or wellness-centered space that brings people together through food, presence, and community.

Three Years of Learning to Be Enough: One Day, One Recipe is his debut memoir — written not with perfection in mind, but with the hope that someone, somewhere, will feel a little less alone.

You can find more of his work at @kinnick.lately on Instagram.